T0304882

The Pocket Photographer

How to take beautiful photos with your phone

Mike Kus

Laurence King Publishing

First published in Great Britain in 2021 by
Laurence King, an imprint of the
Orion Publishing Group Ltd
Carmelite House, 50 Victoria Embankment
London EC4Y 0DZ

An Hachette UK company

10 9 8 7 6 5 4 3 2

A CIP catalogue record for this book
is available from the British Library.

ISBN: 978 1 91394 768 2

Design and Illustration: Mike Kus

Printed in China by Prosperous Printing Co., Ltd.

Laurence King is committed to
ethical and sustainable production.
We are proud participants in
The Book Chain Project
bookchainproject.com®

www.laurenceking.com
www.orionbooks.co.uk

Contents

Cameras don't take pictures, people do

Open up any photography magazine and you'll be told that it's all about cameras, lenses, sensors, aperture settings, etc. And it is about these things. But more than anything, it's about you. Photography is about how you see and experience the world around you. Ninety-nine per cent of what makes any photograph a success is you. It is, by far, the creative decisions that you make that will have the greatest impact on the photographs that you take, and not the type of equipment that you use.

What does this mean? Well, first, it means that you don't need a fancy camera. Second, it means that you shouldn't be put off by a lack of technical photography knowledge; that will come in time.

This book aims to level the playing field and show you that anyone can be a good photographer. All you need is yourself, your phone and a pocket.

1.0

Composition

Every photograph is a combination of three main ingredients: composition, light and creativity. Each of these ingredients plays an important role in the outcome of every picture that you take.

We're going to start by looking at composition. A composition is, by its very nature, also a combination of ingredients. In terms of photography, a composition is the arrangement of objects – a consideration of vantage point, depth, perspective and scale. All of these ingredients exist in every picture, but you get to choose how they're arranged. In this chapter I'll show you how to take advantage of each of these compositional ingredients so you can create balanced, interesting and engaging photographs.

Quick tip:

If you rise early, not only are you able to capture your landscape in the beautiful morning light, but there's also no one around. A location like this quickly gets busy in more sociable hours.

Other techniques used:

01: Shot in early-morning light (golden hour).

02: Eye-level vantage point.

03: Using the perspective of the pathway.

1.1

Build depth & balance

It's the visual arrangement of objects and elements in a photograph that gives a picture a sense of depth and balance. To create a genuine sense of depth, we need to create a composition that has multiple layers: a foreground, midground and background.

This classic view of the Coastguard Cottages and the Seven Sisters in East Sussex, England, already has these three layers. We have the road in the foreground, leading to the cottages in the midground and the Seven Sisters fading away into the background. All we have to do is stand there and shoot.

We don't always have the luxury of natural compositions like this in our day-to-day lives, but we can use these principles of composition everywhere we go. It's just a case of being aware of your surroundings and looking around for ways to layer up your photographs to create that depth and balance.

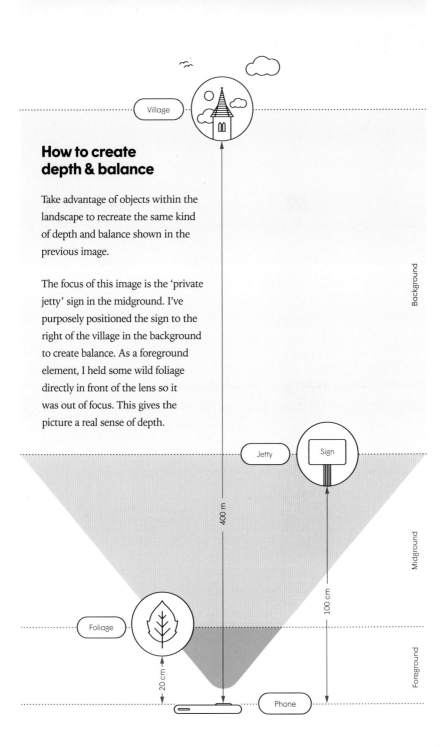

How to create depth & balance

Take advantage of objects within the landscape to recreate the same kind of depth and balance shown in the previous image.

The focus of this image is the 'private jetty' sign in the midground. I've purposely positioned the sign to the right of the village in the background to create balance. As a foreground element, I held some wild foliage directly in front of the lens so it was out of focus. This gives the picture a real sense of depth.

Village

Jetty

Sign

Foliage

400 m

100 cm

20 cm

Phone

Background

Midground

Foreground

Quick tip:

Whilst building your composition, think about the texture and detail in the objects you're bringing into frame. The addition of objects with intriguing details and character will add yet more interest to your image.

Other techniques used:

01: Photographed from low vantage point.

02: Shot in the golden hour (just before sunset).

03: Increased Warmth by 20% in editing.

Quick tip:

When you're photographing a landmark in an open space, look around you to see if there's anything to frame your photograph in the foreground. It will add that depth and balance, and bring focus to your subject.

Other techniques used:

01: Taking advantage of the snowy weather.

02: Muted colour tones in editing.

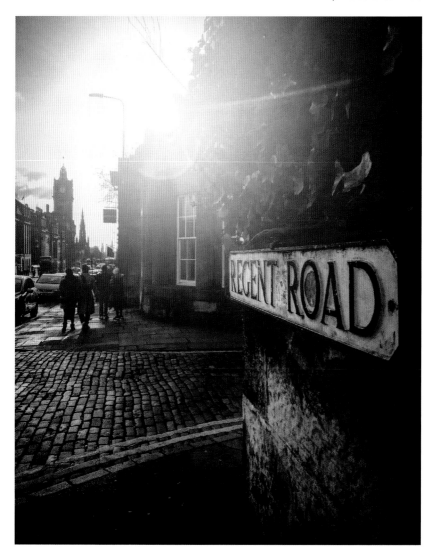

Quick tip:

Something as simple as a street sign can bring the foreground interest that you're looking for. As well as contributing to the balance of your composition, it also adds context.

Other techniques used:

01: Shot in the early-evening light.

02: Using the perspective of the street sign.

03: Framing the sun for flare.

1.2

Find new vantage points

We all see the world from an all-too-familiar vantage point. It looks unsurprising and maybe even boring. Fortunately, there are countless other vantage points from which to view the world around us. Imagine you're an insect ascending a blade of grass; what does the world look like from there? I tried to recreate that viewpoint in this photo, and it turns out it looks pretty cool from down there. When we take a photograph, we have the chance to show a different view of the world and it's amazing what impact an alternative vantage point can make on your photograph.

I always try and shoot from an unexpected vantage point because it makes for surprising photographs.

Quick tip:

By getting your camera deep into the grass, you'll benefit from various parts of your image going out of focus. This will create a symphony of colour and texture, as well as a bokeh effect on out-of-focus dewdrops.

Other techniques used:

01: Creating a bokeh effect.

02: Shooting in low-level sunlight.

03: Macro photography.

Work your arms & knees

Overhead

Hold your phone up as high as you can and photograph your surroundings. You'll be surprised by how different the world looks from just a couple of feet above your head.

Eye level

Taking shots from eye level will give you a realistic view of the world. This is fine for many subjects, but this viewpoint is a common one. Try shooting from alternative vantage points to give you more interesting results.

Mid level

Taking shots from a mid-level position subtly changes your view and brings objects that sit below the horizon closer together, vertically. This has the effect of adding more detail and interest to the lower part of your image.

Low level

Taking shots from ground level will give you a dramatically different view of the world. Turn your phone upside down so the lens is closer to the ground and share a perspective of the world that people rarely see.

Quick tip:

When you're in the city, you need only to look up to find a great vantage point. Use the perspective of the city's supersized architecture to create unique photographic compositions.

Other techniques used:

01: Using perspective of sculpture and buildings.

02: Distorting the scale of juxtaposed objects.

03: Creating a balanced composition.

1.3

Lead with perspective

Perspective exists in every photograph we take. It's what gives the two-dimensional photo its sense of depth, height, scale and proportion. But it's possible to use perspective in a more overt fashion to create bold and eye-catching pictures.

This picture was shot between two beach huts. The lines that lead into the centre of the picture help guide the viewer to the subject and convey a sense of depth.

Try shooting down a long, straight path, or photograph a winding road as it tails off into the distance. There are all sorts of scenarios in which you can use perspective in a more obvious way to achieve this kind of effect.

Quick tip:

If your phone has one, try using the wide-angle view. This greatly exaggerates the sense of perspective within your picture as it squeezes much more of your surroundings into the frame.

Other techniques used:

01: Making use of the light between the huts.

02: Shot at the widest angle possible.

03: Vignette added to draw focus to subject.

Quick tip:

Don't be afraid to photograph the same location over and over again. With each visit comes a different kind of light, and maybe a different season. It might be the same place, but it will never be the same photograph.

Other techniques used:

01: Shot in early-morning sun and haze.

02: Using tree shadows as part of composition.

03: Increased Contrast and Clarity in editing.

Quick tip:

When you're photographing a road or path that tails off into the distance, experiment with where you stand in order to frame the shot. Just a few steps either way can make a huge difference to the composition.

Other techniques used:

01: Taking advantage of autumn colours.

02: Mid-level vantage point.

03: Vignette applied to darken edges.

Quick tip:

When you're in the city, the compositional relationships between objects such as statues, monuments and buildings makes for interesting photos. Look out for unique vantage points that tell a story.

Other techniques used:

01: Simple composition.

02: Addition of Vignette in editing.

1.4

Tell a story with scale

The closer we stand to an object, the bigger it appears. This is because it takes up more space in our field of vision. If you hold a penny up close to your eye, it will look bigger than a car that is ten metres away. When taking photographs, we can use this to create interesting relationships between objects.

In this photo, I used this technique to make the statue of Winston Churchill in Parliament Square appear as large as Big Ben (Elizabeth Tower), which sits approximately 125 metres behind and 90 metres above Sir Winston. Not only does it create an interesting visual effect by distorting the scale of these two objects, it also inserts some storytelling into the image. In this case, the scale of Churchill in relation to the iconic clock tower suggests an imposing character.

How scale works

This diagram shows how the previous photo was created. The closer we stand to the foreground object, the larger it will appear in relation to the background object (Position 02). We can maximize this effect in composition by juxtaposing objects that have a meaningful relationship with each other.

Position 01:

By standing further back we reduce the size of the foreground object in comparison to the background object.

Position 02:

The photograph on the previous page was taken from this vantage point.

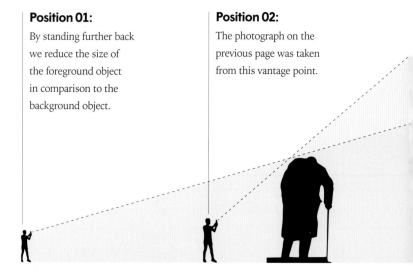

Quick tip:

Combining the effects of vantage point, perspective and scale can result in powerful and unique compositions.

2.0

Light

Light is everything in a photograph. Light is colour, shadows, texture and atmosphere. You can take the same photograph a thousand times and get a different result on each occasion, all thanks to the light. Sometimes the light can work against you, but mostly it's your friend. Learn how to work with the light that's available to you. This will enable you to produce pictures in almost any condition and transport the viewer to that very moment in time.

In this chapter, I'll take you through the different ways you can use light in any given situation. Through these simple lessons, getting the best from the available light and being creative with it will soon become instinctive.

Quick tip:

An added bonus to early-morning sunlight is mist. Be on the lookout for this combination of light and mist, as it can transform the landscape around you.

Other techniques used:

01: Using shadows as part of the composition.

02: Taking advantage of the morning mist.

2.1

Golden hour

Unless it's really cloudy and grey outside, the time of day you take
your photographs will have a dramatic impact on the outcome of your
pictures. Taking photographs in the middle of the day when the sun is
high in the sky can be difficult; it floods the world with light, shortens
dramatic shadows and strips away the textures and details that the
early-morning sunlight exposed.

Shooting in the morning or evening when the sun is low in the sky
is a brilliant time to take photographs – that's why the first and last
hours of daylight are called the 'golden hour'. The low-angled light
creates vibrant colour, shadows and textures. It adds a natural filter
for your shots, bringing a unique atmosphere to your pictures that
can only be achieved at these times of day.

Quick tips:

The obvious benefits of golden-hour light are the dramatic, multicoloured skies, long shadows and beautiful textures. But sometimes the morning light brings with it a more subtle atmosphere.

Don't overlook those hazy, misty mornings when the light comes in cooler tones. This kind of environment produces photographic results that are every bit as good as photos that are shot in that golden hour light.

2.2

Low sun, long shadows

One of the great benefits of taking photographs when the sun is low in the sky is that objects within the landscape create long, dramatic shadows. As they are not physical objects within your surroundings, shadows can be easy to overlook, but you can use them to great effect to produce striking compositions. The shadows cast by objects can be just as important to the outcome of your picture as the light itself. Shadows bring out the textures of the various surfaces within your photograph to add a layer of extra detail.

Shadows also help bring shape and purpose to the light. By shrouding parts of your photograph in darkness, shadows allow the light to draw the viewer's attention to the focal point of the image.

Quick tip:

In bright sunlight, line up your subject to block the direct light from the sun. Treat the shadow as part of your composition. You can do this with a tree, person or building to create bold and dramatic imagery.

Other techniques used:

01: Mid-level vantage point.

02: Using the low-angle sunlight of morning.

03: Simple, uncluttered composition.

Quick tips:

As well as using shadows as part of your composition, think of what they bring to your images in terms of the textures, patterns and atmosphere.

By adopting a mid-level vantage point (crouching height), the foreground shadow cast by the tree opposite takes up a larger portion of the frame, allowing us to take advantage of the natural perspective it creates.

Quick tip:

In the above picture, I used a low vantage point to bring the long grass into the foreground while maintaining focus on the transmitter tower. This adds another layer of interest to the photo.

Other techniques used:

01: Foreground grass adds depth.

02: Dusk shoot.

03: Using multicoloured sky as the backdrop.

2.3

Silhouettes

Photographing silhouettes is an easy way to create a dramatic image that's full of intrigue. The reason this technique produces such good results is because less is often more. In creating a silhouette, we remove the details and distractions, and insert a layer of mystery. The image gains a sense of story. It invites the viewer to add their own interpretation of what is going on in the photograph.

To create a silhouette, simply photograph your subject with the light source behind it rather than in front. It helps when the light source is low in the sky. If the light source is too high, it will light up your subject. Photographing your subject in front of an evening sky is a good place to start. Take a look at the diagram on the following page to learn how best to create a silhouetted photograph.

How to create a silhouette

The ingredients for creating a silhouette are pretty simple: a light source behind your subject and an uninterrupted background.

You can see from the diagram below that anything within the subject area, whether it be a person or a landscape feature, will make for a great silhouette. Your single light source could be from a window or the glow from the setting sun, as in the photo opposite.

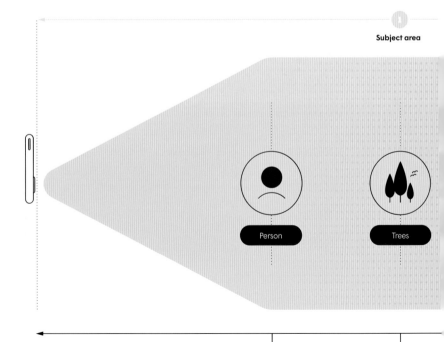

Subject area

Person

Trees

3 m

30 m

Shooting silhouettes at sunset

The light behind your subject does not need to be bright sunlight. A great time to shoot silhouettes is just after the sun has gone down. There's still enough light behind your subject to create the silhouette, and the sky is often multiple shades of red and orange at this time. It makes a great backdrop for your silhouette to stand out from.

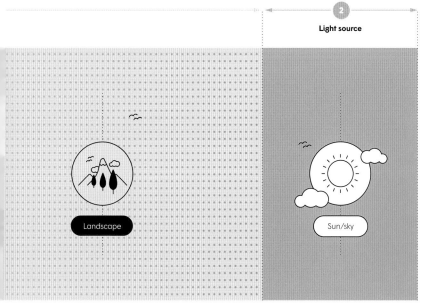

Light source

Landscape

Sun/sky

Infinity

Distant landscape

2.4

Window light

The light from a doorway or window can be used in many ways to produce poetic and atmospheric photographs. What at first might seem like a very normal scene can be transformed by a flood of light that pours through a doorway or window. Images that might otherwise be dull and two dimensional are filled with atmosphere, narrative, questions and nostalgia.

In practical terms, having some light coming into the scene from a window is great for taking pictures indoors without the need for flash, which would strip the image of atmosphere. There are also numerous creative options available to you. Window light is great for still lifes and portraits, and you can also use a window or doorway to frame your subject.

Quick tip:

Light from a doorway can create a lot of shadows and texture. You can boost these by experimenting in black and white and increasing the Contrast. It can add extra detail and interest to your photo.

Other techniques used:

01: Simple, symmetrical framing.

02: Converted to black and white.

03: Increased Contrast.

04: Vignette added to bring focus to centre.

Quick tips:

Light from a window, doorway or any kind of opening can produce shadows that create beautiful patterns and textures.

As with shadows, treat the light that enters the space as part of the composition. Be mindful of the form the light takes and build it into your photo.

Quick tip:

Using a tree canopy to disrupt the light is a great way to bring atmosphere to your photograph. The canopy above breaks up the light to create shadows and textures on the ground below.

Other techniques used:

01: Using the perspective of the pathway.

02: Vignette added to accentuate tree tunnel.

03: Warmth increased in editing.

04: Colour saturation increased in editing.

2.5

Dappled light & mist

As we've learned, shooting in the middle of the day when the sun is high in the sky is difficult; the light is brutal and can strip your surroundings of any atmosphere. However, there are ways around this. The shadows from a tree canopy create a patchwork pattern of broken shadows on the ground below, and this dappled light can help bring atmosphere, detail and texture to your picture on days when the sun is super bright.

Another time in which sunlight is disrupted to great effect is on a misty morning, as seen in the images on the following page. Not only does the mist soften the bright morning rays, it also gives the light a physical presence and exposes its direction of travel. Obviously, as a photographer you have no control over the weather conditions, but capturing photos in the mist can produce some amazing results, so it's worth being ready with your camera on these mornings.

3.0

Lenses

Since phone cameras first appeared on the market, they've come a long way, and the tech and hardware are constantly being improved. If you own a modern phone, you've probably noticed that there are two or three lenses on the back. As well as the standard wide-angle lens, many phones feature an ultra-wide along with a telephoto lens. The telephoto lenses are generally capable of 2–5× optical zoom. This allows you to zoom in on your subject whilst keeping image quality high. The picture opposite was taken using a 5× optical zoom. It is possible to zoom in even farther, but this uses a digital zoom and there is a loss in image quality.

Most modern phones also feature a Portrait mode, which enables the user to simulate a shallow depth of field similar to what can be achieved with a dedicated camera. The end result gives you that lovely out-of-focus effect in the foreground and background whilst maintaining focus on the subject.

3.1

Angles of view

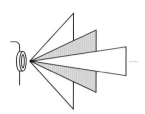

Each lens on your phone has a specific angle of view that makes it a good choice for particular situations.

The default, wide-angle view is good for most situations – general-purpose shooting where you want your photo to have a natural perspective.

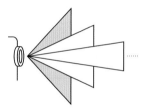

The ultra-wide lens is great for when you're trying to capture an epic vista or you're struggling to fit your subject into the frame.

The telephoto lens allows you to get closer to your subject. It's great for zooming in on a landmark or person when you're just that bit too far away to capture them using the standard wide lens.

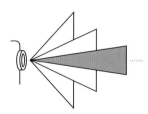

Wide angle

This is what you'll see when you open up the camera app, and by not calling attention to itself, it lets your subject do the talking.

Ultra-wide angle

Many modern phones now come with an ultra-wide lens that is great for dramatic effects, as well as fitting more in the frame within tight spaces.

Telephoto

Not only does this make a faraway subject larger, it's also helpful for cutting out unwanted distractions at the periphery of your image.

Quick tips:

All of the above images were shot using an optical zoom set between 2–5×. This has the effect of pulling together elements at different distances and making them appear closer together within the frame.

The image opposite was shot using the ultra-wide lens. Shooting at this low vantage point shows just how much we're able to fit into the frame: everything from the main subject to the leaf, just a few inches from the lens.

3.2

Macro photography

Macro photography means shooting small objects or details and reproducing them so they appear large in your frame. Not all phone cameras have a specific Macro mode, but all are capable of close-up focus. You can photograph the tiny details and textures of a flower, shoot close-up shots of insects or capture beads of water on a leaf. Macro photography opens up a whole new world that is rarely seen in everyday life.

Taking a macro shot

Zoom into your subject until you've reached the maximum optical zoom, taking care not to extend into digital zoom. Hold your phone as close to your subject as possible without the image going out of focus – this will be just a few inches away.

As you're very close to your subject, you might find the focal point jumps around. Tap and hold the part of the image you'd like to focus on until AF LOCK appears on the screen. This will lock the focus onto the desired area.

Whilst framing your subject, also consider the background, as small changes of vantage point will cast your subject against very different backdrops. A contrasting colour or darker background will help your subject pop out.

Good lighting is essential for macro photography. Shoot where there's plenty of natural light to bring out the detail, colour and texture of your subject. Macro photography is all about these details.

Quick tip:

For a magical atmosphere, shoot in the golden hours of the morning or evening. It works particularly well when the colours of the subject reflect that of the golden light.

Other techniques used:

01: Low and close-up vantage point.

02: Out-of-focus background.

03: Shot in the golden hour.

4.0

Focus

While it's important to capture your main subject sharply in focus, out-of-focus areas can add depth and a feeling of mystery or romance. They can also help you draw attention to a certain part of the image whilst softening the peripheral details. This is generally achieved by using what is called a shallow depth of field.

Put simply, depth of field is the distance between the closest and farthest objects within your photo that appear in focus. A 'shallow' depth of field is when this distance is short. You see this technique used widely in portrait and food photography, wherein the focus is locked on a certain part of the image whilst the foreground and/or background remain out of focus. It's easily achievable with a dedicated camera, but trickier with a phone. Due to the physical limitations of a phone camera, the natural depth of field is very deep, meaning that almost everything remains in focus. Fortunately, there are ways around this.

4.1

Selective focus

Whilst the depth of field of your phone camera is deep, it's not infinite. Try placing objects very close to the lens; the camera isn't capable of keeping both the close foreground objects and the distant background in focus at the same time. This enables you to achieve either an out-of-focus foreground or background. Simply tap on the area of the screen where you'd like to maintain focus. Depending on which part of the image you have chosen to focus on, this will force either the foreground or background of your image to fall out of focus.

I've used this technique in the photographs on the opposite page. In the main image, I chose to focus on the grass in the foreground, thereby giving me an out-of-focus background. With the inset image, I chose to focus on the village in the background, which gave me the blurred grass in the foreground.

This technique makes the most of the physical limitations of a phone camera. To create the shallow depth of field you can achieve with a dedicated camera, you'll need to use your camera's Portrait mode. This simulates a shallow depth of field using the phone's software. I'll take you through this feature in the following pages.

Quick tip:

Touch and hold the part of the image you'd like to focus on until you see AF LOCK. This will lock your focus and stop your camera's autofocus from focusing on different parts of the image.

Three ways to achieve selective focus

The diagram below shows three different areas of focus that, when selected, give you out-of-focus areas in other parts of your image.

SHARP FOREGROUND, BLURRED BACKGROUND

In order to achieve an out-of-focus background using a phone camera, place an object in the extreme foreground, such as grass. Select the grass as the focal point of the image (**Focal area 1**) by touching the grass on the screen. This will blur the background of your image.

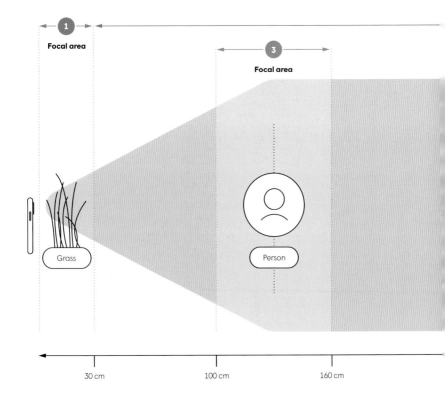

Focal area

Focal area

Grass

Person

30 cm   100 cm   160 cm

BLURRED FOREGROUND, SHARP BACKGROUND

To achieve an out-of-focus foreground we simply do the opposite. We bring the grass into the foreground and select a focal point in the background (**Focal area 2**). This will blur the foreground of your picture.

PORTRAIT MODE: THE BEST OF BOTH WORLDS

Using your phone's Portrait mode, we can simulate the shallow depth-of-field that's achievable using a dedicated camera. Standing a few feet away, select your subject as the focal point (**Focal area 3**). This will bring focus to the subject whilst blurring both the foreground and background. See the examples on the following pages for more details.

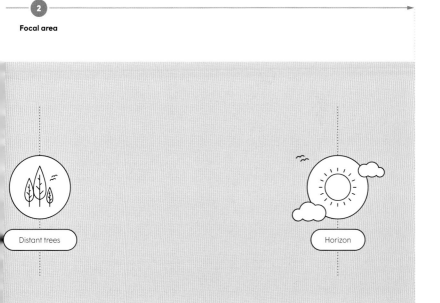

4.2

Portrait mode

Due to the physics of a phone camera, the kind of shallow depth of field you see in the main picture opposite isn't possible without the help of software. When your subject is a few feet away from you, this falls into the area of the image where everything remains in focus (as in the inset photo). To combat this, manufacturers introduced Portrait mode. Almost all modern phones now integrate this feature.

Using clever computational analysis, Portrait mode is able to reproduce the shallow depth of field that normally requires a dedicated camera. It gives you the power to isolate your subject from both the foreground and background, softening any unwanted background distractions and bringing focus to the subject of your picture. It's a powerful feature that's easy to use without any technical photography knowledge. This brings you another step closer to producing the kind of photographs that you'd expect to see from an experienced photographer using a professional camera set-up.

Quick tip:

Your subject needs to be at a mid-range distance for Portrait mode to work properly, otherwise your phone may give a message telling you to move farther away.

Quick tip:

In addition to shallow depth of field,
Portrait mode can also create a range of
lighting effects, similar to filters, that mimic
professional studio lighting equipment.

Other techniques used:

01: Convert to black and white.

02: Addition of Vignette.

03: Increased Contrast.

Quick tip:

Creative cropping to focus on a specific facial feature can make for a unique portrait.

Other techniques used:

01: Increased colour contrast.

02: Addition of Vignette.

03: Increased Clarity.

Quick tip:

Turn your phone upside down and bury the lens into dew-covered grass. The out-of-focus dewdrops will produce a beautiful cacophony of bokeh circles.

Other techniques used:

01: Ground-level vantage point.

02: Early-morning sunlight.

03: Abstract composition.

4.3

Create a bokeh effect

When points of light are rendered out of focus by a shallow depth of field, they appear as luminescent circles called 'bokeh'. Sprinkled across your photograph, these out-of-focus floating orbs can add a layer of magic to your picture.

Try photographing water droplets on grass or flowers. You'll need to get right up close to your subject, as the key is to make sure some of the droplets are out of focus. Each of these droplets will act like a tiny light bulb, creating balls of light that collectively produce the bokeh effect. Tap your screen in different places to change the focal point; this will in turn alter the kind of bokeh the camera captures.

As an alternative to a close-up bokeh effect, try creating the same effect by using the lights of a city skyline (as shown on the following page). Focus on a foreground object to force the city lights in the background out of focus. The busy cityscape will transform into a soft backdrop of lovely bokeh lights.

Quick tip:

In the above image, I locked focus on the foreground bridge railings to force the background city lights out of focus. When you're shooting at night, be sure to keep your phone steady to avoid camera shake.

Other techniques used:

01: Unique vantage point.

02: Used foreground element as a frame.

03: Focus locked on foreground.

5.0

Think creatively

The one tool in a photographer's toolbox that trumps any technical knowledge is the ability to think creatively. Being able to spot great photo opportunities is what will have the biggest impact in helping you build a portfolio of great images.

It's easy to visualize a potential photograph whilst standing in front of an epic vista, but we don't always have such exotic subjects available to photograph. Luckily, there are photo opportunities all around us every day; we just need to have our eyes open to them.

It can often feel like you're out of ideas when snapping your local area, but there's always a different creative take. Look for that unique vantage point, capture images in reflections, add objects into the foreground to create depth, get creative with light, shadows and texture. Keep different creative approaches in mind to turn your local surroundings from the ordinary into the extraordinary.

5.1

Frames within frames

We're used to always seeing our local surroundings from the same point of view. Use what's around you to create images with an alternative perspective. Here are some ideas:

Tree inside tree

Sometimes you stumble across unique viewpoints created by nature. Not only does this old tree provide a unique frame, it also offers the perfect view beyond.

Props

Use what you have on your person to help you produce creative and fun images. When you're all out of inspiration, experimenting with props can lead to some great pictures.

Fence view

Photograph through the railings of a fence or gate. It's a unique vantage point and you can experiment with the focal point. Choose between bringing focus to the foreground fence or the background landscape.

Round window

This view through a ship's round window provides a unique viewpoint and creates a striking contrast between the dark interior of the ship and the sunshine and blue sea beyond.

Quick tip:

There are no rules when it comes to being creative with your picture-taking. The more experiments you do and the more alternative viewpoints you try, the more likely you are to get some really interesting results.

Quick tip:

Sometimes the natural geometry of your
composition will frame your subject. Notice
how the house on the left, the pathway and
the wall on the right-hand side frame and
draw focus to the subject of this photograph.

Other techniques used:

01: Increased Contrast and Saturation.

02: Cropped and centralized.

03: Geometric composition.

Quick tip:

Keep your eyes peeled for alternative viewpoints from which to photograph your surroundings. They're not always obvious, but they are often right in front of you.

Other techniques used:

01: Using the perspective of the canal.

02: Out-of-focus foreground.

03: Heavy Vignette to draw focus to the centre.

5.2

Check your reflections

Whether you stumble across a street scene in a car's rearview mirror or notice a local landmark reflected in a puddle, using reflections to create dramatic and otherworldly compositions is definitely something you should try.

Whilst it's possible to go out in search of reflection pictures, more often than not they're sprung upon us by chance. And since we'll almost definitely have our phones to hand, we're perfectly placed to seize these opportunities.

Photograph your own rippled reflection in a rainy-day puddle. Capture your home city, town or village as it's reflected in the river. Simultaneously capture cityscapes and urban life in the windows of cafés or bars. There are endless reflection opportunities. Be ready to take advantage of them when your chance arises.

Quick tip:

A sharp reflection in still water will instantly create a unique and surreal composition. Take it one step further by rotating it upside down to create an otherworldly, brain-melting photograph.

Other techniques used:

01: Framed from a mid-level vantage point.

02: Shot in early-morning mist for atmosphere.

03: Photographed in autumn colours.

Quick tip:

Shooting through a window reflection lets you overlap interior and exterior scenes to create a full story in a single frame.

Above I used my phone's ultra-wide lens along with a low vantage point in order to fit the full length of the trees and their reflections into this photograph.

Quick tip:

Keep in mind the compositional elements of
vantage point and perspective, and always
try to shoot in the best light of the day.
These strong fundamentals combine with
reflections to make extraordinary images.

Quick tip:

To create this image, I positioned myself
opposite my subject and shot her reflection
in a pool of water, producing an upside-
down image. I then rotated it in editing
so that my subject was the right way up.

Other techniques used:

01: Playing and experimenting.

02: Increased Saturation.

03: Increased Contrast.

Quick tip:

In this picture, my aim was to create a bold and simple composition. I also used the low-angled morning light to accentuate the shadows and patterns created by the veins of the leaf.

Other techniques used:

01: Focus on leaf for out-of-focus background.

02: Simple and symmetrical composition.

03: Increased Warmth in editing.

5.3

Celebrate the simple things

The temptation is to look for obvious beauty within our surroundings – gorgeous landscapes, captivating portraits or iconic city architecture. These are all good choices, but you don't need access to these to take great pictures; you can capture the simple things instead.

Photograph a leaf. Think about shooting the details we so often miss. Use the morning light to help reveal the leaf's detailed network of veins. Photograph shells washed up on a beach or capture the beads of dew on a newly formed spider's web.

Photographs of simple objects are no less valuable than epic landscapes. Simple things can be beautiful pieces of art in their own right. And it's often the small details that act as a powerful or poignant reminder of a bigger story or a certain place and time.

Quick tip:

Photographing simple objects and details throws up a wealth of new opportunities. This creative freedom can help push your photography in an experimental direction.

Other techniques used:

01: Early-morning hazy mist.

02: Making use of reflections.

03: Balanced, layered composition.

5.4

Capture autumn's colour

Each season brings with it new colours, light and atmosphere. In my mind, the top spot has to go to autumn. As the summer fades and the nights draw in, nature puts on its most spectacular colour show, giving us endless photo opportunities.

For a few weeks in October and into November we can really make use of the autumn colours on display. Photograph the amber-filled streets, capture the texture of leaf-covered pavements or hold up a fallen leaf to the sunlight to reveal its texture and vivid colour.

One of the other major advantages of shooting in autumn is that sunrise and sunset happen at a much more sociable hour, meaning that as well as the awesome colour display, we have the beautiful morning or evening light in which to capture the autumn setting. For a triple bonus, look out for misty mornings. The colour, light and mist together make a great combination.

Quick tip:

You might find that the colours in your images appear less vibrant than they do in real life. Play with the Saturation, Tint and Warmth tools to enhance the colour that was lost in the original photograph.

Other techniques used:

01: Mid-level vantage point.

02: Using perspective of road to create depth.

03: Increased Saturation and Warmth.

Quick tip:

Shooting the autumn leaves along a road or pathway enables you to capture layer upon layer of colour and texture as the trees and foliage tail off into the distance.

Other techniques used:

01: Pathway perspective drawing focus to centre.

02: Increased Saturation.

03: Addition of Vignette.

Quick tip:

Without the distractions of colour, images can take on a stronger, graphic quality, emphasizing shapes and textures over conventional subjects.

Other techniques used:

01: Close-up photography.

02: Out-of-focus background.

03: Cropped composition.

5.5

Black and white

In a world of flashy LCD screens with ultra-wide colour gamuts, black-and-white photography still has a special magic. Stripping the colour from your photograph pushes it one step back from reality, instantly giving your image a sense of history and nostalgia. Black-and-white pictures remind us what photographs are: snapshots in time that cannot be returned to. For me, this is what makes black-and-white photography so emotionally resonant.

There comes a creative freedom when shooting in black and white. Without colour, there are fewer choices to make, and with fewer choices comes less deliberation.

Try shooting in black and white and see where it takes you. Rather than converting your pictures to black and white after you've taken them, select a black-and-white filter to shoot with. This way you're actually viewing the world around you in shades of grey as you take your photographs.

Quick tip:

There's an automatic emotional draw to photographing people in black and white, but it's also worth experimenting with landscapes. You can achieve some really striking, cinematic results.

Other techniques used:

01: Perspective leading viewer to centre of image.

02: Vignette to bring focus to subject.

6.0

Night vision

In recent years, photographing the night has become a fiercely fought battle between the major phone manufacturers – all of them tout their low-light capabilities. Advances in technology and software have meant that huge strides have been made into this space. Thankfully, they've done a pretty good job; all the modern phones I've tested have returned impressive results.

Night photography is an art form in its own right, and it takes you to different places – literally. At night, you're either chasing the light from the moon and stars or the artificial light created by humans. Once the sun sets, these lights are what guide you – street lamps illuminating the pathway below, the glow emanating from the windows of the city's restaurants and bars, neon signs, rippling reflections of light in puddles and rivers, the white and red streaks from passing traffic, the moon and the stars. These are the light sources that will illuminate your night-time photographs.

6.1

Creating sharp, well-lit night pictures

When shooting with Night mode, it can take anywhere from one second to a full minute for the phone to finish taking the picture, so it's important to keep very still to avoid shaky images. It is possible to take hand-held night photographs, but you'll achieve much sharper results if you secure your phone in place. You can do this by simply leaning your phone up against a solid object within your surroundings, but this gives you fewer options as to where you can take a picture from.

If you enjoy night photography, it's really worth investing in a mini tripod. They're super light, compact and you can fit them into a coat pocket. I use a Manfrotto PIXI and attach a phone clamp. It's a great piece of equipment that makes night photography much easier.

You could also use the flash but I much prefer to capture night scenes using the light available. It achieves more natural results.

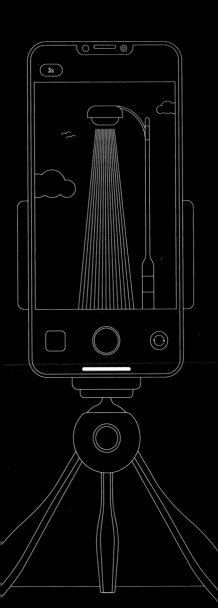

Use a tripod

Using a tripod for your night shots not only keeps your phone steady, it also allows you to be very precise with your framing.

Softly, softly

Even small movements of the camera can result in shaky, blurred images. When you press the button to take your picture, be careful not to wobble your phone.

Capture time

Less light means the photo will take longer as the shutter stays open to receive enough light ('exposure') to produce the image. Some phones let you choose exactly how long.

To capture a well-lit street scene, you might need only a few seconds. If your aim is to capture light trails, you might need anything from five seconds up to a minute.

Quick tip:

Unless you're shooting the night sky, urban
areas are the best for night photography.
Look for spots where there is a medium
amount of human-made light – architectural
lighting, street lamps and window light.

Quick tip:

To create a photo similar to the one above, frame your picture and secure your phone in place. You'll need 30 to 60 seconds to capture light traces over this kind of distance.

Other techniques used:

01: Phone on tripod and locked in position.

02: Shot on Night mode.

03: 50-second capture time.

Quick tip:

Architectural lighting gives enough light
that the picture will take only a second or
two, so it's possible to hand-hold this kind
of shot. To avoid camera shake, lean against
something solid for extra stability.

Other techniques used:

01: Foreground foliage to help framing.

02: Out-of-focus foreground.

03: Balanced and layered composition.

Quick tip:

This isn't strictly a night shot. It's very early morning just before sunrise. This is a great time to capture some low-light atmosphere. You don't need to shoot on Night mode either; this was a standard hand-held shot.

Other techniques used:

01: Shot using 2× optical zoom.

02: Photographed just before sunrise.

7.0

Your life

The beauty of phone photography is that you always have your camera with you. Each and every day, new photo opportunities will take you by surprise, and you'll always be ready to capture these moments. It's the lifestyle you lead and the people you spend time with that guide your photographic work. Your portfolio will be a reflection of your life – it will tell your story.

We all lead different lifestyles with our own unique experiences, and we'll all choose different moments to capture. My life is family life; I'm based in a small city that's close to the sea, surrounded by countryside, and my pictures very much reflect this. In this chapter, I want to touch upon some photographic subjects that are less prevalent in my body of work but might be more relevant to yours.

7.1

City streets

There are over ten thousand cities across the globe, each like a humming organism full of diversity, culture, colour and atmosphere. For all you city dwellers, there are just as many, if not more, photo opportunities surrounding you.

The city is perfect for street photography. Capture the scale, traffic, signage, graffiti, city lights, people and pace of life. Street photography offers you a new photo opportunity with every step you take. And with the convenience and ease of use that comes with a phone camera, it's the ideal device on which to record these moments.

Photograph the architecture. Capture the juxtaposition between the old and the new. Look straight up to shoot the extreme perspective created by the city's buildings as they race upwards towards their vanishing point. Every city has its own personality and unique stories to tell. Tell the story of your city.

Quick tip:

The concrete architecture, free-flowing graffiti, light, textures and skaters combine perfectly to capture this urban street scene.

Other techniques used:

01: Motion blur caused by movement of skater.

02: Increased Contrast.

Quick tip:

City streets offer a labyrinth of nooks and crannies. The limited light available in certain locations often delivers some really interesting photos that can create atmospheric urban photography.

There is no shortage of skyline photographs available to you in a city like New York (opposite). Try shooting in black and white to create a sense of history and nostalgia.

Quick tip:

Candid moments happen so quickly that you need to be ready in advance. When you predict a genuine smile is coming, pre-frame the shot with your phone at the ready.

Other techniques used:

01: Using optical zoom to help blur background.

02: Using Portrait mode.

7.2

Friends & family

When we think of portraits, we often picture someone sitting for the camera, the subject's face and smile; but a portrait can be much more than that. A portrait can tell a story. The combination of the subject, the location and perhaps a specific moment in time can produce an image that is more powerful and meaningful than the sum of its parts. When we photograph our families and friends, we do it to capture memories. We bottle them up in a photograph for us to look back on and be reminded of their personality and the times that we've spent with them.

There are lots of ways we can capture these memories, and you can be as creative as you like with your portrait photography. Try shooting candid shots of your friends or family to capture their personality; photograph your kids in a certain location that adds meaningful context to the picture; photograph through windows, capture reflections, freeze movement. There are no rules.

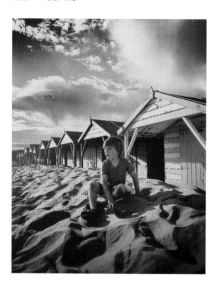

7.3

Storytelling

Sometimes a single image is all you need. However, by creating a collection of images, you're able to tell the whole story. Each image in your collection builds on the last, adding more information and context. The end result is a set of images that tells a vivid narrative of a place, person or time.

With a collection of photographs comes a certain creative freedom. You're no longer forced to choose that single shot that best represents your subject. You can be more relaxed about your photo choices. You have the luxury of being able to capture some of the details that you might ordinarily skip over. It's these details that give the viewer a more intimate insight into your chosen subject.

Presenting a collection of pictures will enable you to convey real atmosphere with multiple layers of emotion, and ultimately help you tell the whole story.

Quick tip:

Don't labour too much over photographic choices. The luxury of creating a collection of images to tell a story is that no detail is too small or insignificant. They all contribute to communicating your experience.

Other techniques used:

01: Photographing small details.

02: Capturing the simple things.

03: Using multiple vantage points and framing.

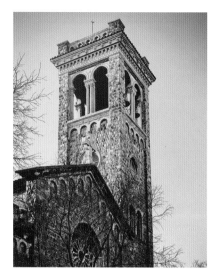

Quick tip:

Capturing something as simple as a sunlit building's texture or some local street art goes a long way to communicating what it actually feels like to be in a city. All these small details matter.

8.0

Editing

Your phone can take well-lit, high-quality images. But due to the obvious physical limitations of a phone camera, there are limits as to what can be achieved in comparison with a dedicated camera. Luckily, we can address many of these limitations with a few simple edits. Most phones come with a comprehensive suite of editing tools, and there are plenty of apps available to help us enhance our photographs.

With the editing tools available, we can bring warmth to our pictures, improve the colour and soften the light. These enhancements help us recreate the atmosphere of what it was like to be there at the time. For me, this is the main objective of photo editing: to bring the viewers of your picture on the journey with you. The edits you make to a picture have the potential to help transport the viewer to a certain place and time. Let this objective guide your editing process.

8.1

Universal editing tools

Whether you're using your phone's built-in editing suite, Instagram or any other app, there are a range of editing tools that are universal across most photo-editing applications. Here's a brief breakdown of the main adjustment tools – what they do and how they can enhance your photographs.

Crop & Straighten

It's common to look back through your pictures and realize that your horizons are not perfectly straight, or some unintended object is intruding into the frame. You can correct these easily with the Crop or Straighten tool. To straighten, simply rotate the image until the overlay grid lines up with the horizon. To crop, zoom into your image until the distracting element isn't in frame – you can drag the frame after zooming in to adjust more precisely. Don't zoom in too far though, or the resulting image will have lost image quality.

Adjust & Geometry

When photographing architecture, especially a tall building, you'll notice that they lean in to the centre of the image. This can be fixed by using Keystone correction – more commonly referred to in editing apps as Adjust or Geometry. On most phones it's found within the Crop or Straighten tool. By using this tool you can adjust inward-leaning verticals and make them straight again.

Contrast, Shadows & Highlights

Contrast is the difference in tone between the dark and light areas of your image. If you increase the Contrast, the dark areas (shadows) get darker and the light areas (highlights) get lighter; if you decrease the Contrast, everything flattens out towards a middle grey. The Shadows and Highlights tools control these two areas independently from each other. You may want to lift the Shadows of an interior when shooting the outside from within, or decrease Highlights to make clouds visible in a bright sky.

Saturation & Vibrance

The level of Saturation determines
the intensity of the colour within your
pictures. Lowering the Saturation makes
colours more muted, whilst increasing it
makes the colours richer and more vivid.
It's very easy to go too far, however, and
push your colours into the garish and
unrealistic. That's why you also have the
Vibrance tool. Whilst Saturation affects
all colours equally, Vibrance affects only
those that are muted, leaving already-
vivid colours alone. This prevents you
from pushing the colours too far.

Warmth

The Warmth control can either make
your photograph feel warmer or cooler.
Increasing Warmth brings out the
amber/yellow tones, and decreasing
the Warmth brings out the blue tones.
Sometimes your phone returns a cooler
image than you expected, so you can
put back the warm tones into the image
by increasing the Warmth. It's great for
emphasizing that golden sunlight you
experience during a sunset.

Tint

Tint works in a similar way to the Warmth tool except that you're pushing the colours towards either magenta or green. If you're shooting under human-made light, you might find your picture has a yellow or greenish tint to it. You can remove this by pulling the Tint slider towards the magenta side.

When your image's colours seem off and unrealistic to the scene, a combination of Tint and Warmth will often let you correct this and achieve realistic results.

Sharpening, Definition, Clarity & Structure

The Sharpening tool helps crisp up slightly fuzzy images. It's useful, but should only be used sparingly as it can bring unwanted noise to the image. Increasing the Definition, Clarity or Structure accentuates detail and adds a three-dimensional quality. It's good for enhancing textures and making objects pop, but pushing it too far can make your image feel grungy and rough around the edges. Decreasing these tools has the effect of smoothing out fine detail, which can be flattering for portraits.

Noise Reduction

Noise (a mottled texture) is normally noticeable in the larger, empty areas of your image, such as the sky. Some natural noise in your picture is fine, but sometimes it can detract from the serenity of certain photographs. The Noise Reduction tool can fix this. Be careful not to push it too far, as it can soften other parts of your image where you would like the clarity to remain.

Vignette

Applying a Vignette adds a soft, dark halo around your picture. You can adjust the size and strength of your Vignette, and as always, subtlety is key. You should be able to apply an effective Vignette without it being obvious to the viewer. It's a great tool for reducing any peripheral distractions, drawing focus to the central subject and building an atmosphere.

Brightness & Exposure

The Brightness and Exposure tools control how bright or dark your image appears, but they do it in different ways. Brightness affects all the tones in your image, brightening or darkening the shadows along with the highlights. Exposure, on the other hand, affects only the highlights, leaving your shadows alone.

Grain

This tool replicates the grainy texture you might see in a picture taken with a film camera. In digital photography, the addition of Grain is an aesthetic choice; it can add a certain emotional resonance. It simplifies the image by bringing focus to the subject of the photograph rather than the technical qualities of the picture itself.

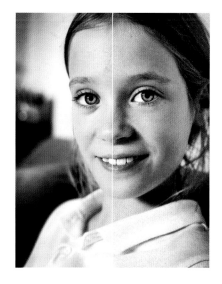

8.2

Editing sequences

Let's go through a few editing sequences that take a photograph from its original state through to the end result.

Original picture

The exposure is a little uneven due to shooting into shadow that's blocking the sunlight. The horizon line slopes down the right, and the image is lacking the warm, golden atmosphere that was present at the time.

Edit 01

First, we can straighten the horizon of the image by using the Adjust or Straighten tool. We can also lift the Shadows to even out the exposure.

Tree edit

In this editing sequence I want to accentuate the sunlight pouring through the branches of the tree and bring the warmth back into the image that was lost in the original photograph.

The edits in this sequence were done using my phone's native editing tools and Instagram, but you can use any photo-editing app with similar features.

Edit 02

Some phone cameras tend to output slightly cooler tones, so I've increased the Warmth of the image to replace those golden tones that were lost.

Edit 03

Finally, I have increased the Vibrancy to heighten the colour and texture of the photograph and I've brightened the image to accentuate the light flooding through the branches of the tree.

Misty street edit

In this editing sequence, I add a twist to a misty street reflection scene. I'm using my phone's standard editing suite and Adobe Lightroom for mobile to make these updates.

Original picture

The buildings look slightly wonky due to the low vantage point this picture was taken from. The misty grey morning has also zapped the colour.

Edit 01

My first edit is purely one of fixing the Geometry. I've tilted the image very slightly to the left and corrected the alignment so the buildings on the right look straight.

I mentioned in the introduction to this chapter that, when editing, make it your goal to recreate the experience of that specific moment. However, there are no rules when it comes to editing pictures, and I'd encourage you to be as creative as possible. Try new editing apps and new techniques, and take inspiration from other photographers. By experimenting, you'll find that you develop an editing style all of your own, one that's unique to you.

Edit 02

I've increased the Warmth and Vibrance of the image here. I've also boosted the Saturation of the yellow lines using the Color Mix tool in Adobe Lightroom, and added a little Sharpening and Definition to bring out the detail.

Edit 03

For my last edit I've added a slight Vignette and adjusted the Tint very slightly towards magenta. For a final twist, I've also rotated the image so that the reflection is on the top.

Black & white portrait edit

In this editing sequence I aim to capture the personality of my subject and create a nostalgic-feeling black-and-white portrait. In this edit I'm using my phone's native editing tool and Adobe Lightroom for mobile.

Original picture

This photo was shot on a summer evening with the light low in the sky. While I think this works quite well in colour, I can see an opportunity to make a more evocative black-and-white portrait.

Edit 01

I first crop the image to bring focus to the subject. By moving the subject up and to the right it gives the photograph a more natural feel whilst also cropping out the church steeple in the background.

All modern handsets come with a pretty good set of photo editing tools. But there are also a multitude of great apps available in the major app stores.

Many third party apps offer more specific editing capabilities that allow you to alter your image in ways that your native tools can't achieve. It's worth playing around with these apps to see how they can contribute to your editing process and the final outcome of your pictures.

Edit 02

I then converted the image to black and white. You can do this by either choosing a black and white filter or lowering the Saturation tool to zero. I've lowered the Saturation to zero, in preparation for some final edits.

Edit 03

Finally, I made a few adjustments to the black and white image. I've increased the Contrast and also the Shadows to make the image feel more dramatic. I've also increased the Clarity and texture in the image to bring out the small details.

One last thing

I hope this book has given you some knowledge, ideas and inspiration for you to go out and start capturing your surroundings from your own unique perspective.

Whether you're a professional or a hobbyist, photography brings with it exploration, enjoyment and creative satisfaction. It enables you to express yourself and share a view of the world in the way that you see it. In some ways, the end result is for other people to enjoy, but the process and art of creating the pictures along with the experiences you have whilst photographing them are all yours. This is the true enjoyment of being a photographer and it's open to anyone.

As I said at the beginning of this book, photography isn't about the equipment you use – 99% of what makes any photograph a success is you. All you need is yourself, your phone and a pocket.

Glossary

Background: the part of a photograph farthest away, often forming a backdrop to the main subject (p.8).

Black and white: an image consisting entirely of black, white and grey tones, with emphasis given to shapes and textures, often with a nostalgic quality (p.100).

Blur: any part of a photograph that is not sharp – this can be the result of being out of focus (outside the depth of field) or subject motion (too fast for the capture time to freeze) (p.66).

Bokeh: the result of points of light being captured outside the depth of field, resulting in bright circles in front of or behind the main subject (p.76).

Candid: a type of portrait taken spontaneously, often without the subject's knowledge, resulting in an informal, realistic portrayal (p.118).

Capture time: the time it takes the camera to record an image – shorter in bright conditions and longer at night; also called 'exposure time' or 'shutter speed' (p.107).

Composition: arranging elements of a scene within a frame, giving consideration to vantage point, depth and balance, to achieve an aesthetically pleasing representation (p.7).

Contrast: the difference between the darkest and brightest areas of a photograph (p.129).

Crop: the act of zooming in and rotating an image, deleting peripheral objects and making the main subject larger in the frame (p.128).

Depth of field: the distance between the nearest and farthest objects in focus. Images with 'shallow' depth of field will have out-of-focus areas; those with 'deep' depth of field will be sharp from front to back (p.64).

Digital zoom: the range beyond 'optical zoom', synonymous with cropping – best avoided as this always decreases image quality (p.55).

Filter: a preset series of edits that can be applied to a photo, often recreating a particular look or style.

Focus: the distance at which you decide objects should be sharpest and attention should be concentrated (p.65).

Foreground: the part of the photograph closest to the camera, often in front of the main subject; elements are placed here to add a sense of depth (p.8).

Golden hour: the first and last hours of sunlight, during which the colour of light is rich with reds and yellows, and the angle is very low in the sky, resulting in long shadows and high-contrast textures (p.33).

Grain: originally the mottled texture resulting from processed film, now recreated using digital techniques to focus attention away from technical perfection and towards the subject's emotional resonance (p.133).

Image quality: a combination of sharpness, resolution and colour accuracy that represents the best that the camera's technology is capable of.

Macro: a type of photography that makes small subjects take up the entire frame by focusing at close distances (p.60).

Midground: the area between the foreground and background, usually where the main subject is located (p.8).

Night mode: a method of taking bright photos in dark lighting conditions that requires long capture times, during which the phone must remain absolutely still (p.106).

Optical zoom: the range of angles of view that a given lens can provide without any loss of image quality – usually in the telephoto range of 2–5× (p.55).

Portrait mode: a method of using computational analysis to recreate the shallow depth of field that dedicated cameras are capable of; requires the subject to be a few feet away from the camera (p.72).

Saturation: the intensity and purity of colour in an image; a photograph with no saturation will have only shades of grey, whereas a highly saturated image like a sunset will have an abundance of colour (p.130).

Sharpening: the digital method of adding fine detail to edges in an attempt to cover up any detail lost to blur (p.131).

Telephoto: a lens with a narrow angle of view that pulls distant objects closer so they fill the frame, and in doing so, compresses the space between objects at various distances (p.56).

Vignette: the effect of darkening the edges of a frame so that attention is pulled towards the centre; can be of varying levels of darkness and reach (p.132).

Warmth: similar to saturation, but concentrating only on red and yellow tones, often used to recreate the golden hour (p.130).

Wide angle: a lens that fits large, nearby objects into frame, and exaggerates the space between objects at various distances (the opposite of a telephoto) (p.56).

Acknowledgements

I'd like to thank my amazing wife, Em, for her support, patience and being on hand to sense-check my writing every five minutes. Thank you to my kids Theo, Olive and Jonah, not only for being the subjects in many of my photos but for your constant enthusiasm and willingness to help me out. Thank you, Mum and Dad, for your support; and thanks, Dad & Jock, for giving the book the once-over and correcting my errors.

Thanks to my family and friends for your encouragement and friendship over the years.

Finally, thank you to the team at Laurence King, especially Zara, Melissa and Alex, for your expertise and guidance.

Where you can find me:

Instagram: @mikekus
Twitter: @mikekus
Web: mikekus.com